VSW 2003

Iodine

or,

A Visit to Jake's Kero Confectionery
during the Elks' Rodeo Parade, 1963

for Jack

in admiration
of your passion,
conviction, quickness
and intelligence
that sees through
smoke to the heart

Harold

Iodine

or,

A Visit to Jake's Kero Confectionery During the Elks' Rodeo Parade, 1963

Harold Rhenisch

Harold Rhenisch

Wolsak and Wynn . Toronto

Cover art by Harold Rhenisch
Author's photograph by Diane Rhenisch

The publishers gratefully acknowledge support by The Canada Council and The Ontario Arts Council.

Typeset in Times Roman, printed in Canada by Coach House Printing Company, Toronto.

Wolsak and Wynn Publishers Ltd.
Don Mills Post Office Box 316
Don Mills, Ontario, Canada, M3C 2S7

Canadian Cataloguing in Publication Data
Harold Rhenisch, 1958-
Iodine
Poems.
ISBN 0-919897-40-1
I. Title. II. Title: A visit to Jake's Kero confectionery during the elk's rodeo parade, 1963.

PS8585.H46I63 1994 C811'.54 C94-931255-X
PR9199.3.R45I63 1994

for Diane

CONTENTS

ONE JUNE AFTERNOON AS THE HEAT BLOWS IN WAVES THROUGH THE VALLEY

Lord, thou art great, thou art
the mosquito who gnaws its way in
through the screen!

We used to slow to a crawl
on the road to Cawston

If we looked east
we could see the twisted metal
and junked cars
of the welding shop
at Vickner's corner

If we looked west
we could smell
the Natural Gas Pumping Station
trembling behind its chain-link fence

Now we drive with our feet pressed to the floor

Now when family come from the Old Country

we drive out into the sagebrush
until the wheels spin

then we shut the engine off

and listen
to the sun walking through the grass

far away

and the grass crackling

We know it has taken a long time

  but we have seen the German Shepherd
  hide under the bed

  as the thunder picked the house up
  and tried to shake her out
  like a child with a piece of gravel in a pop-tin

and we know now
that one can look too closely on the world

SALT LICK, IODIZED

The Goddess

        has squeezed herself into her magpie suit

The Goddess

        is burning from head to foot

and you

        lord of dust and airfilters

are kicking around in back of Quaedvlieg's ranch pickup
up the alluvial fan of Barrington Creek

        When they heave out the dead cow
        among the others there

you leap off

As the pickup rattles down
again to the steel-roofed barn

you wait among the old bones

        She comes too

with her long black beak

        doing the breast stroke through the air

her whole body trembling

    for it's dinner time
    up on K-Mountain!

You've brought her some scraps

    just some old stuff you don't need around any longer I
    guess
    isn't that right did I guess right?

Late that night when she is cold
and the moon is raging within her
with its tides and its heavy water

    she comes again

in her coyote stole

    the fur wrapped right over her face
    against the night wind

she comes through the rocks and the purple-flowered knapweed
skittish

    like a shadow

    and You are there
    asleep
    wrapped up in an old cow-hide

She nudges you with her cold nose
Like a small child you wake up
and stare at her

        from two inches away

She startles
then laughs

        We have you wrong
        we thought you were a shotgun shell
        heavy in the pocket

but you are a salt lick

        you are the bales of barbed wire
        shiny and oiled
        in the back of Similkameen Farm Supplies
        with the fertilizer and the Chicken Grow Crumbles

and the deer come to you
and lick

OUR LORD WALKS DOWN MAIN STREET IN SURPLUS, VIETNAM-ISSUE BOOTS

The sunlight on the snow
is a joyful blindness

And the water that breathes out the water
is the violin that cries out for the violin
but is blind to itself

Just so do men
call out to their god

to teach them how to hammer a scythe
how to stroke it

so it does not snap off
at a single blade of grass

and just so does he hone them

with his indifference

Each moment he suns on the gravel bars of the river
without them
in the long light of September

rings out

the sound of stone howling over metal

and they grow sharp

and cut

    And all the time
    that men spend
    turning the keys

in the ignitions of their pickups

    all that time every day
    all that wonder and release

he sits at his Father's side
and plays protest music
from the sixties

    in the rotten plastic deck chair on the front porch

and that is praise enough

    for as he walks past the angels
    their copies of Awake!
    held over their hearts as shields

we are laying our heads on our Dacron II pillows

angry at all the things we haven't got done!

As he walked down the street
the dogs burst up crying as he passed,

like women at a long funeral service,
with the Father sipping the wine
and the altar boys whispering jokes;

and the mothers drew away their children.

He stood there in line with the others,
the Indians, the teenage mothers,
the violent, the drunk and the battered,
paid by the state just like him
to maintain order,

all the old gods and the fallen angels,
pressed right up against the door of the Valley First Credit
Union,

all singled out for shame.

Outside, all the dogs
were drooling into the dust
outside their plywood doghouses, in their boredom,
waiting for him to return —
as they knew he must — and they could sing

like a choir and a Wurlitzer organ

and the organist in bare feet
so she could caress the pedals
and through them her Lord God of Song-O.

COMPASSION

First the words

        and then a sort of flowering Yucca

with the petals as white as a porcelain fixture

        in the morning sun!

First the inarticulate
cloud chamber of thoughts

        where each word burns
        like a spent rocket booster

        and falls to the seabed

with the angelfish and the slow, languorous kisses
of used condoms

        each with its own little puddle of memory!

Then the contrition

        the cardboard Renoir
        above the little girl's bed

in a cardboard frame

        the articulation of lust

the simpering body

WHEN THE APPLE JUICE IS PRESSED UNDER THE BIRCH TREE WE HAVE TO COOK THE DANCE OUT OF IT QUICKLY

He is our god

and we are white-tailed deer

startling in a thicket

our ears huge, uplifted

listening hard for the slightest sound

and where there is none

But, lord, that's where you come in!

HYMN FOR HERBICIDE

Consider for a moment the water strider
that skips across the surface of the water

held up by the tension

held up by the love of water

for its own kind

So do we throw the plastic jugs of Roundup
in the backs of our pickups

along with the broken bits of PVC pipe
and the blow torches

and the rusted clippers!

because there's couchgrass under the trees
It's got them by the trunks

Because there in that black oil and dioxin
you are hiding

At one kiss of your lips

the grass turns brown and withers

We are two of a kind
we've got to stick together

Do not leave us alone
in this desert of mock orange and cactus

Stay with us
cling to our faces like a cloud of dust
fill our lungs

    We're just 12-year-old kids
    out discing the fields in April

    thrilled to be so dirty and so tired

Fill our lungs with dust
grind the enamel off our teeth
it's nothing

You are great

    You are the mercury fillings

dissolving into the bloodstream

    of the 32-year-old nursing mother

and the iodine sprayed on the bunchgrass

    for mile on mile on mile

above the moon-grey waters
of the Columbia river

    draining out to the Pacific!

HYMN FOR SMALL ENGINE REPAIR

As the feller longs for virgin timber

        and the moss crackling underfoot

So do we long for our lord

and as the pipefitter longs for Saturday

        so he can wake up beside his wife
        and turn over to hold her

        because his skin feels like sheet metal

and his bones like galvanized iron

        so does *our* god
        long for lightning all night
        and white rain in the morning

so he can watch all the farmers get up
and walk around aimlessly, waiting

        not knowing what to do

with such freedom!

        So does the god of the fouled sparkplug

open up a small engine repair shop
in the weatherbeaten garage behind his trailer

It is perfect!

right down to the *Briggs and Stratton* sign
nailed above the door
and the rusted lawnmowers

strewn around through the cactus
and the sagebrush

When I sit down and think on it
I want to weep

Because when the people start to come

in their nylon-mesh hats with the sun-faded brims
their pickups bouncing over the shale

and drag their broken machines before him

I want to see him come out
of his dark doorway

Because I want to see the pity in his eyes

I want to see how he handles it

when his people return to him

I want to be *there*

Highway 3

There was a woman riding a horse
on the gravel shoulder. The horse looked at him with pity,

with the bit in her mouth and the saddle
cinched up around her gut. He looked at her with pity too:

in his dreams the devil sat on his back
and whipped him on the bare buttocks

until the blood ran and he began to weep in Spanish
about revolution and replanting his cocaine fields with coffee,

to keep people awake half the night and restless,
and then they put the electrodes to the glans of his penis

and hooked him up to the corroded car battery
until he lost consciousness and it was morning,

and the sun was on the streets outside
like spilled engine oil, and flies, and hungry children.

The horse saw it too, and the skin all down her flanks rippled,
a shudder passing back from her mind through her whole body,

and she flicked her tail
and stamped her feet.

Giddyap said the woman in the saddle
and dug the spurs into her flank

and pulled hard on the bit
so it pinched her on the lips. Giddyap!

The wind lolled on the trembling flank of the mountain

The whole valley stretched below her
blue and smoky like a trench on the sea-floor

        and she dreamed

her breath rising and falling

        scented with pine pitch
        and wild low-bush blueberries

two hours to fill a red
plastic beach pail!

        that he had come to her there
        three thousand feet above the valley floor

banging rocks together to scare away bears

        and shouting

at the top of his lungs

        Glory glory glory
        to the electric can-opener!

and she thought

        she had never heard such singing

and grew hot and restless with it

    Down below in the valley
    the shingles tore off the roofs

the wind spilled over the garbage cans
behind the houses

    and sent the children running indoors
    their nylon windbreakers flattened against their chests

Our lord of baking soda and vinegar

    we wake up slowly one morning
    in late August
    When we go outside

it is fall
the apples are lying in the grass
the apple trees

    are lifting up their arms to the wind

    the wind is brushing through them

    lovingly

so tenderly do you come

    full of milk cartons
    pressed up against the roses

with the last trace of milk in them

all sour

just so do you come
bless us wrap your arms
around us tenderly

just so do you come

with nothing in your mind but us

who have nothing in our minds at all

except the wind

that is blowing

down the small rain

THE BATH

for Gary Snyder

He would ride down
the dusty road under the moon,

through the bruised grass
of the orchards,

in the hours of the first frost
and the tungsten starlight,

his face burnished like molybdenum,
the valley road as dark as coking coal;

and slip into the wooden-floored showers
of the pickers cabins

below Barcelo Road, wash, ride back
up the gravel driveway

to his mountain,
the dust caking again to his face like slag;

and he took it with great silence
and courage —

and he would load his pockets
with the half-ripe apples.

Back in his cave,
he would bite into them:

their sourness and hardness
would mix in his head

with the smell of dog-shit,
the smell of life itself —

a ripeness before its time;
the dead crow hanging by its foot in the doorway,

turning on the orange binder twine
on each twist of the wind.

And in his dreams the wind sang
Holy Holy Holy is the Lord Dog our God.

PSALM: GRAB A WHISK BROOM AND SWEEP A PATH BEFORE OUR REDEEMER

For he is the broken pane of glass
with the condensation between the panes

        in the dining room!
        The tax notice
        I understand now I have seen it all!

the non-refundable Tax Credit

        the Vaseline
        on the windowledge above the changetable
        that we dip our fingers into
        and smear on thickly

For blessed are the children

        They shall come to him

For they are strainèd carrots

        like lambs in a green meadow

and love

        the milk running hot down their chins!

We are the tiny clay men
walking at the bottom
of the poisonous sea of the air

SUNDAY SHOPPING

Up at the Keremeos Regional Refuse Disposal Site,
he saw a TV, grey with cellulite,

staring at him with open thoughts.
"What do you want," he asked of it,

for it seemed to be staring directly at him.
"I want sugar," it said. "I want sanctimony,

and I want you to pay me in cash."
It smiled. "Father," he answered back,

"When do I wake from this dream?"
But the screen was dead and blank.

It was starting to rain. The crows
settled out of the air,

suddenly, and began to argue and tear
at his thoughts — scattered all through the trash:

grapefruit rinds and the hind leg of a goat,
and a sheep-hide rotted by the rain,

and a bicycle tire-pump crushed in half,
and a mattress with a broken back,

stained with blood.
And he understood.

THE HERALD TRUMPETS OF THE LORD!

Materials needed: empty paper towel rolls, breath

Awake!
    For the lord can't fit the new battery
    into his $3 digital watch

    and he's going to take it out
    on the first person he sees!

Awake in sorrow!
    He is bankrupt
    and has slipped strips of cereal boxes
    into the soles of his boots

Awake!
    He is almighty
    and we are like potato beetles to him
    eating his main crop

    so ugly
    he doesn't want to touch us with his fingers

Awake in anger!
    The lord has risen late
    and staring out the window
    in his frayed terrycloth bathrobe
    has given him a headache
    and he's in a bad temper
    and there's no more coffee in all
    the Autonomous Republics of Heaven!

PSALM, FOR ENNUI

A Self-directed RRSP

For ours is the self-effacing god

There is the goddess of the moon
and the holy sows of the earth

    but ours is the god of Nothing
    and Emptiness and Death

He is all our own

    The great Zero!

The pro-rated battery warranty!

    The pregnant teenage mother!

The VSE.

WHAT WAS LOST HAS BEEN FOUND, WHAT HAS BEEN FOUND IS LOST

One of the earliest records
of the Incarnation

dates back to the year of breathlessness
Nineteen Hundred and Seventy-six,

when he was pruning in an orchard owned by an Alberta oilman
on the old ranchland

at the base of Fairview mountain,
wrestling with the trees

in a thin, crusted snow, but unable to shape them,
unable to form them

into an image of his mind,
the branches and the root,

for whenever he went to cut a limb,
high up there on his ladder in the silver snow,

there would be an angel sitting on the limb
in a heavy parka, its hands in its armpits

to keep warm, calling, "Hey, watch out there,
why're you cutting *that* branch off?"

He'd look to the ground: there'd be more angels there,
clustered at the base of his ladder,

their breath freezing before them
like Players cigarette smoke.

"You want to leave some fruit on the tree, eh!"
And they'd chuckle amongst themselves. Every time,

there were more angels underneath him,
stamping the snow into a fine powder

that the wind sprayed up from around their feet,
pointing to his work, laughing.

From the edge of the orchard
still more of them would be walking in — the snow swirling up
over them

as if they were images of carbon monoxide.
When the newcomers started to *run*

in through the overhanging, overgrown trees,
he could no longer see the point of resistance.

"What do you want with me?"
They laughed. "Well, there's so damned many of us, these days,"

a tall one said, halfway up the ladder behind him,
grinning. All the others stood silently and still,

like elders at a memorial gathering of Ukrainian Germans,
staring — some holding their mitts to their ears,

to warm them. "What else are we supposed to do?
We used to do our work ourselves,

but now we're underemployed
and between situations!" A brief flicker of pity

came through his frozen, blue face. "Besides,
a guy's gotta have some reason

to get himself out of bed in the morning,
and today you're the only thing happening for miles!"

He looked over the group, that stretched out
all around him, and formed his thoughts slowly,

the way a young woman rolls her first cigarette,
and then licks it, so her tongue

tastes of paper. They looked like a bunch of sheep,
hanging their heads down,

their urine steaming up over their faces
as the snow settled on their backs. "Day's over,"

he said, and stepped down the ladder,
out of the Starking Red Delicious tree,

and through them. They parted to make a path for him,
with the snow clotted in his beard

and his toes frostbitten in his boots; and clapped
as he passed through, the heavy

leather sounds of their mitts
thumping on the air, like a man

pounding a dog's back so the dust flew up
as the fleas scrambled for cover;

and closed ranks behind him;
and followed him out of the orchard,

chatting amongst themselves, laughing,
dreaming of hot coffee. Behind them

the snow sifted through the branches
and the matted couchgrass

and the frozen apples in the grass;
and on the small twigs

in the centres of the trees
held perfectly still, like choked sobs,

and bled light,
all through the settling dark.

For our lord suffers the children
to come unto him

Praise to him that he may avert war
amongst us

He changes a word here and there
in what they have to say to him

Praise to him that he may avert war
amongst us

So they will not be understood
Not even by other children

Praise to him that he may avert war
amongst us

For that is the suffering
that is ever the lot of men

And the wasteful abundance

And the sorrow

Praise to him that he may avert war amongst us!

As the years went by
he grew more violent,

more closed in on himself
there on the mountain,

among the rocky mountain maples
and the BC Hydro Transmission Line;

and the farmers down in the valley
would lean against the tailgates

of their Japanese pickups,
and shake their heads:

"I worry for the children.
He's an accident waiting to happen."

Then they'd go on to their favourite
topic of conversation —

how on the old Plester Place
they'd found that missing French girl

last week, buried in the greenhouse with the torn plastic
all milky and snapping at the wind,

but without a head,
it had been chopped off with an axe, eh,

and you can't prosecute the guy who did it
if there's no head, shit,

and later, in bed, with the lights out,
their women would say do you think so?

laying their cold hands on their men's chests, to warm them,
how could anyone do such a thing,

I don't understand it. The men would hold them close
and not say what they'd felt:

that there's nothing to understand:
it's as easy as putting on a pot of coffee,

or changing the oil in the tractor
every 300 working hours,

the cold touch of the steel clinging to your hands;
feeling that there was some shame in understanding.

High up on the mountain, where the moon burned
like a car with only one headlight,

the other smashed out by a Highways sanding truck
down by Richter Lake, the lord of miracles

dreamed that a young girl came up to him,
dressed in jeans and a wool sweater,

stood in the entrance to his cave, and pleaded with him to save
her,
but she didn't say from what:

when he woke from his dream
he saw three men standing over him;

before he could rise
they beat him with 2x4s and one length of metal pipe,

and left him there, and smashed at the dogs as well
on their way out.

Then one of them turned and spoke
before disappearing into the light:

"Stay away from my sheep!"
When he woke, he was bruised and bloody,

but could remember none of the beating,
only those last words, and they puzzled him,

for there on that mountain of ozone and soapstone
there were no sheep.

OUR LORD IS A BLISTER IN THE PALM OF THE HAND, OUR LORD IS A ROCK

When we think of our lord
our eyes brim with tears

and the mites at the roots of our eyelashes
come out, shyly, to drink

When I think of our lord
the lord of the Lace Teddy
and the Wire Support Brassiere

I confess my gratitude

When I think of our lord
the god of the Spermicidal Jelly
and the Stimula Ribbed Condom

I confess my pleasure

When I think of our lord
the god of the Real Estate Developer
and the Hydrostatic Transmission
my eyes well with tears

And I sing Hallelujah the lord has come!
He has given me a sign!

For the lord is the Three Buoys Houseboat Vacation

The UPC label

    And Carole Martin Direct Mail Advertising

And I sing my gratitude

    For the lord is the Cantina
    of the 1x6 Cedar siding
    and the lava rock

Rejoice at the Burnt-out Lawnmower Muffler

    For that too is our lord

The very rivetting Hammer of Impatience!

    The son of the Working Classes!

The No-name Brand Beer

    The small-mouthed bass!

THE NIGHT RAID

On one windy night
in the years of our domination,
dogs broke into the sheep pen
of old loading pallets wired together,
just down from Brian Mennell's
on the sloping gravel benchland
of the Fairview Heights Second World War Veteran's settlement
and snapped the necks of the two
month-old bottle-fed lambs,
and left them there in the dark straw,
under the scrap-aluminum stars;
and lunged for the ewe;
tearing her matted, unshorn hide
off her quivering body,
from her shoulder back to her belly.

Hearing the noise, Brian struggled down
through the chicken shit and the old batteries
and the tractor parts
and shot at it with his 22,
but he didn't get them,
and they were gone
into the throat of the night.

High on the mountain, as the coyotes called to each other
through the windy pine forests
and the woodticks clung on to their grassblades
for the second month of their springtime,
dark grass sighing and twisting in the night
like scrap metal — with his dogs curled up against him,

rank, greasy, unwashed,
but warm and bony, and scratching themselves ocassionally
with a ridiculous gusto —
our lord woke at the report of a gun and the scream
of an animal in intense pain.
There was no more sleep left in him;
his whole body was tensed, charged,
the whole air around him
and stretching down through
and flooding the valley,
and the black water rushing through the bed of the river,
was electric with fear.

Then it came, tattered on the wind: the sound of the second
gunshot;
as the bullet hollowed out the ewe's head;
then only silence, and the wind
thrashing through the trees, throwing its whole body at them,
like a man crashing through the underbrush,
his compass broken, looking for a high point of land,
frantic; tired.

As the dogs slept all around him in a shifting, fetid heap,
he lay awake there among them,
his heart pounding,
his breath just a wisp,
like a flame almost extinguised;
and only at dawn
when the birds started to cry and holler
and laugh and dance in the trees
did he sleep.

HYMN TO BE HOWLED BEFORE THE OPEN CASKET

Lord thou art higher
than the cotyledon
of the Roma Bush bean seed
brushing the light with its lips

    Thou art higher
    than the red-currant bush

leaving her clothes strewn around the yard
in her delirium

    Thou art higher
    than the swallowtail butterfly

thrusting its tongue deep
into the blue dancing vagina of the delphinium

    Thou art lower
    than the dead limbs on the walnut

and I kiss you on the lips.

    Thou art lower
    than the rotten feet of the picnic table

And I kiss you on the lips.

For thou art the strawboss
of death and insurrection

        and pay TV and 4-head video technology

Thou art the god
who stands out by the road
with a toy spider
and a new plastic lunchkit

        for when Diane slips out of her clothes
        in the late evening

you are the housefly that races madly
through the warm shadows of the bedroom
so she runs after it in her nakedness and her grace

        Because it brings you warmth as well

And pleasure

        To see your children hunt you down like that

with a curled-up Ladies Home Journal

        Because you've made your home
        between the two panes
        of the double-glazed window

Our god who rises and flutters
at the softest touch of the light

setting the whole house singing

just for the fun of it

And just for the fun of it you are the shadow
that follows the children
step by step through the grass
as they giggle trying to escape from you

For you fall down in a heap together laughing

You are a father's love

and a husband's tenderness

When a small boy throws stones
into a creek
you catch them with your mouth
and swallow them

The one who released the Secret of Mascara
so you could see it streak!

So you could forget the pain of incarnation

And the glory

the endless unforgiving memory
of the body

Thou art right now with a tall, thin woman
cleaning her childless house

watching the snow drain down the deep ravines
on the mountains outside her windows

the god of the Cummins Diesel
gearing down at 2 AM
on the steep hill into town

shaking all the glass in the windows
as it passes through

and the pregnant wind that races into the vacuum

the miracle of post-natal water-retention
and the episiotomy

And the first gasp of breath

From the morning
right past the National News at 11
and past the Journal

You are there

the Station Identification Signal

The Paid Political Announcement

and the surgical gloves size 10
laid out beside the stirrups

THE PRODIGAL SON II: A STEVEN SPIELBERG, FRANCIS FORD COPPOLLA CO-PRODUCTION

When the disciples were walking back to their nets
and their vineyards, the lord revealed himself

to them. He was wearing Calvin Klein jeans
and a $140 Pierre Cardin sweater,

and they bowed down before him in shame.
The lord laughed: "Rise, and go spread the Good News,

that your lord has died, but now he has risen;
Death is a prisoner in his own kingdom;

rejoice! There is no good and no evil —
I have banished them outside of time!

Rejoice and spread the good news!"
The lord spent the rest of the day among them,

sitting under the ashen olives,
drinking their sour wine, laughing. He seemed

more like a brother to them than ever,
and he held each one closely to him in his grasp

when he said good-bye. The disciples carried the word
to every corner of the desert. Everywhere

the people heard it, in all the villages and the small huts
of the shepherds among the rocks,

there was rejoicing, there was good wine spilt,
and much late laughter; many a child was conceived

in the rejoicing; the sounds of the partying
filled the land and the air right up

to the seat of God. He looked down afraid
and troubled for his son, on his walkabout. In the heavens

there was no laughter, for every glance taken in Death's
kingdom
has a life of its own, every

indrawn breath, every exhalation,
every touch of the fingers to stone,

lives on, splits away into its own wind,
its own stars and its own ocean,

and down there in the violent winds
his son was walking incognito,

trying to gather up the pieces that had left him.
He had very little time,

and the penalty if he failed
was total annihilation.

There was no laughter in heaven.
Down on the earth the wind blew across the desert,

and burned as it struck the face
with the hand held across the eyes, to shield them.

STRIKE!

When the British Columbia Nurse's Union
struck the Penticton Regional Hospital
in June of nineteen eighty-nine,

in the weeks of cold weather
immediately preceding the cherry monsoon,
with the snow drifting across the peaks,
our lord, his leg swollen
and black from the last rattler
to sun itself on Fairview Mountain,
attempted to cross the nurses' picket line
by the automatic emergency ward doors.

Even as the nurses were stepping aside for him,
lowering their pickets,
for a minute —
like the bored young blonde woman
flagging where they're blasting
to widen the highway past Summerland —
he collapsed on the ground out there, delirious;
in the throat of the sunlight.

When he came to
and once again knew himself
as separate from the tiny, unpolished agates
embedded in the tar,
he was lying on a trolley bed,
with a plastic bag of blood dripping into his arm,
and a man massaging the poison
out of his leg. When he tried to sit up
an orderly pushed him back down gently.

When he looked at them
he saw they weren't angels,
they were just men,
no-one he had ever seen before
or would ever see again,

and he was happy,
with that new blood,
happier than he had been for years;

while outside the nurses paced up and down
and poured each other coffee
from their husbands' battered steel-lined thermoses,

that they had taken for the day,
this their day of trial.

Our lord

    the carpenter

comes out of the woodwork

    writhing, white, and blind

Wherever there is a nail
and a hammer

    He is there between them

and wherever there is one hour
between the morning and the evening

    that is from neither the pas de deux nor the stiletto

He is there

    with his brace and bit
    and his claw hammer

He loves nothing better than a young woman

    pulling on her panty hose
    her hairbrush in her teeth

Like the Bata shoe salesman
at Orchard Park Mall in Kelowna
who looks first at a person's feet on introduction
and then only then clasps their hands in his

        Praise him!

Oh we adore him!

        May we never be parted
        from the waiting room
        at the Canadian Tire Service Centre
        in Penticton

For he is there
standing on a carhood up on the hydraulic hoist
with a microphone

        dressed in rhinestones

giving his Elvis impression

        Love me tender!

Love me true!

INVOCATION: APPLE, ROWAN, ASH

Of those last days long after
the coming of trickle irrigation,

when all the thousand names of the lord
had again been collected,

except for a few scraps
in the farthest mountains,

sing in me, O Muse,
lay down for a minute your Pro-choice placards,

and sing
the Apocryphal stories of Dionysus and Apollo,

when the lord was nearly solely the dirt
we walked on, when all things had become the lord,

and there was no more time —
the elect had already been chosen

and their churches blew empty like driftwood:
of that time, O Muse, sing in me;

all is uncertain to us now:
we know not whence we come,

and do not know what to name our children,
who even still grow up trying to sing.

Sing in me, O Muse, that if a few scraps of time
should drift up against me in the wind

like a Supervalu polyethylene bag in the knapweed,
I can fashion of them a shield,

and of the shield against annihiliation, I can fashion a word,
and of the word I can speak of our lord,

whose last human incarnation is living with us here,
up on Fairview Mountain,

as if abandoned, his energy dissipating,
and with my speech I can enter the earth,

which is yours, where the lord dwells now,
with you, soaking his feet in a blue enamel basin

of warm water mixed with Cow Brand
Bicarbonate of Soda.

That is all the god we can understand,
who is and has always been a turned back to us —

because he is the god of time,
and time is always trying to leave, it is struggling and churning

and now it has done it, it has curdled;
and he is like a worm in the cheese,

and we are like styrofoam cups and paper napkins
left after a picnic in the Cathedral Lake Provincial Park Picnic
Site,

and we walk in our sleep. It is of these
I would have you sing, O Muse, who must speak for him now,
in consternation,

who is smaller than the tent-caterpillar,
who has gone to live with the ants in the birches,

who has taught himself at last how to rejoice!

Two of his oldest, dearest friends
from the garden of the Inquisition
were in the room
when he woke again: Dionysus and Apollo!

They were dressed in tight black suits, white shirts
and narrow ties,
with tightly pressed creases in their trousers.

Apollo was standing at the window,
lifting the corner of a curtain aside with his fingers
to look unseen at the strikers
pacing outside by the cedar bark chips and the 2-4-D
and the rhododendrons.
His tie was black.

Dionysus was sitting at the bedside,
smelling a dandelion
that he had picked outside
as he came in. There was a yellow dust of pollen
on his two-day scruff of grey beard,
and though it should have made him look ridiculous,
it made him look youthful, radiant.
His eyes twinkled.

But it was his tie that our lord couldn't take his eyes from:
it was of a naked women with nipples the colour of a barn door
against a green and gold background!
Dionysus winked, and reached into his vest pocket
and handed him a flask of whiskey.

"Will you cut that out," snapped Apollo, from the window.
"Can't you see our friend here is —"
and he groped for words that would exactly mirror his agitation —
"Unwell?"

But our lord took the flask of whiskey
and he drank from it,
and there was a god in it,
a god of smoke and snow and laughter,
and he swallowed it,
and he fought that god down
until it was as small as a mosquito,
and he looked up at Apollo
weak with the effort,
and laughed.

"Come on," said Apollo. "Enough of this.
We're getting you out of here."

"No," he said, his voice a low drone.
"I like it here. They take care of me good."

When Bill Kinkaid and his brothers
come at lunchtime
in their suits and ties
strangely not sweating
to talk about redemption through resurrection
what then?

Give them a bowl of home-made chicken soup!

If you have none to spare?

Give them a glass of apple juice

If you drank it
just before they knocked on the door?

Speak to them out of that sourness in your stomach
but whatever you do, get them inside
don't let them go!

For they have spoken to the Joiner
And he is making chairs for them in Heaven!

Out of pine and varnish!

Each dowel fitted in by hand!

That is more than the 9 mm tread depth
and the leaded gas

It is the 32 psi maximum pressure
It is the wood curling at the touch of the plane.

HYMN FOR KLEENEX AND A NYLON COMB

Let us now open our hymnbooks
and sign the paean of the whipped cream siphon

O Cholesterol! O Cholesterol!

Let us toughen our hearts against adversity
and breathe the secret name of our lord

Cholesterol, be not proud
We have opened our kitchen cupboards
to the secret name of our god

And he is like a hot water tap among us

and the cabbage loopers
writhing in the catchbasin!

"Hennessy's Cognac, Jameson's Irish Whiskey,"
said Dionysus.

"You think, therefore you are," said Apollo.
He leered at Dionysus.
"You can't just make a list of depressants"

"Glen Livet Single Malt Scotch Whiskey,
Aqua Vit"

"and call that the Incarnation
in the human body!"

"Schloss Kirsch, Mint Schnapps,
Drambuie, Gilbey's London Dry Gin!"

"the dancing of the human body!
Dammit, love and your thoughts shall come clear to you!"

"I couldn't agree more," said Dionysus.
"I drink therefore I am."

Apollo stared at him in amazement.
"Well, whatever," he said,

"but we have to get our old friend here
out of this house of bones and disinfectant."

"I couldn't agree more," said Dionysus,
"but he seems to have fallen asleep."

"He looks drunk to me," muttered Apollo.

"Sleeping like a baby," intoned Dionysus,
his voice low, reverent.

So they got him out of the hospital, under the influence,
supporting him stiffly between them.

"He's light as air," exclaimed Dionysus.
Apollo bit his tongue.

So they got him into Apollo's Jeep Wagoneer 4x4,
and as Apollo turned the key

Dionysus whipped out a bottle of Calvados Père Magloire.
"I'm driving," said Apollo. "No thanks."
Dionysus grinned and tipped the bottle up
to his stubbly old man's lips.

"Hey, save some for me!" said the lord
of Heaven and Earth and Texaco Brake Fluid
from the back seat.
"Don't be so greedy."

Apollo twisted the mirror
to look him right in the face.
"I thought you were asleep," said Apollo.

The young one grinned, wide-eyed.
"He was dancing," said Dionysus.
"That's the whole idea: to instill the body with a fury.
Don't you know anything?"

"Well, I thought you were asleep," said Apollo.
Our lord took the bottle and slung it back.

They drove up Fairview Mountain,
past the old Fairview Minesite above Oliver;
and as the jeep hammered on the washboards,
the pretender rolled down the window
and threw the bottle into the ditch.
It smashed into splinters.

With Apollo driving
and the dust seeping in through the half-rolled glass,
and Dionysus his old friend
imitating Leonard Cohen singing
There Ain't No Cure For Love,

sitting beside him,
as the Jeep threw him from side to side
as they spun out around the sharp corners,

and the pretender in the back seat,
leaning forward, without his seatbelt,
looking out between them,
like a dog sucking in the wind
in the back of a pickup,
grinning,

they pulled up in front of the cave.

At the sound of the doors closing,
the dogs raced out on their leashes:
the leashes snapped them back and again they lunged forward.

"I'm sorry. I don't have anything to offer you,"
said our lord of rusty sheet metal and rotten

mine timbers. "Just a glass of water, maybe," said Apollo.
"We can't stay long, but I've a terrible thirst."

But Dionysus pulled a bottle
out of his jacket pocket, and winked:

"BC LIQUOR BOARD DARK RUM! We don't
need glasses. We can drink it straight out of the bottle!"

But the pretender was not listening.
He had walked amongst the dogs,
and was clasping them to him;
as they leaped up against him,
and licked him on the mouth;

then they knocked him over
and he lay on the ground
and watched the sky seethe drunkenly above him.

"Here, give me that bottle," said Apollo.
"I think we're going to be here for quite some time."

Dionysus handed it right over,
and the lord began to sing

THE SONG OF OUR LORD, or
THERE AIN'T NO CURE FOR LOVE

Dad
        kick off your hiking boots
        and wash your feet
        in the Similkameen River

that drains the sky through us!

        Because there is a worm
        in every bottle of springwater

Because there is a worm
under every pillow

        Because there is a worm
        in every mouth

and we need a rest!

        You can see everything

but we are only a tired crew
at the end of the nightshift

        walking off into the streets of Moscow
        and beating back the Germans
        with our pipe wrenches and sledgehammers

and we need a rest

You're strong alright

like the yellow floodwaters of the Fraser

but we are just kids, Dad
we like the National Geographic

We're tired of books without pictures

We need an afternoon nap!

We found the blind oracular fog

        and thought it was molecular physics

We found the peachleaf willows so heavy with ladybugs
drooping right to the sand

        we thought they were cherry trees

We found Cartesian dualism

        and thought it was a man and his shadow

We found a woman shaving in a shower

        and thought she was a question

Now we have found the light sitting in a robin's nest
in a cherry tree

        eyeing the cat in the grass below

which is also the light!

        Daring him!

and we know

        that the question is the Cartesian dualism

and the man and his shadow

        are the molecular physics

and a woman shaving in a shower

        is a woman shaving in a shower!

A VISIT TO JAKE'S KERO CONFECTIONERY DURING THE ELKS' RODEO PARADE

For the end of the light is the beginning

    All things of this earth shall be reborn
    in man's image

And all the mirrors shall break
in the women's hands

    so they can only see themselves
    in each other

For in life's beginning is death's first toehold

    And in childhood is our salvation

Where we wrestle with Death in the grass
and both fall back laughing!

    Where we chew on red licorice

and it tastes like the body of the lord!

— 1963

This life, this is the song of praise
        the angels carry to the lord

Heaped up in plastic milk crates
        this is the leap of faith!

Not that the lord will come
        his pockets full of Mars Bars!

Not that the lord will come whistling
        at the pretty girls on the street

Tipping his pale blue BC Hydro hard hat
to them!

        but that the lord has come
yesterday and today and tomorrow

        Not that there is any time left to us

Not that the lord is part of an antiquated political system

        But that we have been straining at the ropes
straining at the dimensions!

        putting him to the test!

And he doesn't mind a bit
        He loves to hear people singing!

hallelujah our lord the crocus!
        Our lord the cottonwood pollen

who clogs up the sinuses
        of everyone in town

just like that Hallelujah, our lord has come
He has given us his sign

        nailed to the billboard supports
        at the Similkameen Indian Reserve #2

just west of Keremeos
        Campbell's Soup

Red and White for the Winter Blues!

        Hosannah! Our lord walks naked in the night
        clothed only in our praise

just as we cover *our* beauty
        and radiance!

with rayon and silk and cotton!
        For that is power!

and Playtex bras and Stanfield's jockey shorts
        for that is glory!

For in the end our lord is a 2x4
we drive the nails through it and build a house

for our children!

For in the end our lord is a fencepost

We drive the fencing staples into it so we can string up barbed wires
that the wind can pluck like guitar strings

in praise of him
who too was a country kid

and loved Hereford cattle!

For in the end our lord is a blind god
we take him by the hand

and lead him across the street

and he shies away like a dog at the sound of the cars idling
and we laugh and say those are just cars!

and our lord laughs nervously

like the turbines in the WAC Bennett Dam on the flooded Peace River

in praise of us